C U T A W A Y

FIRE
FIGHTERS

JON KIRKWOOD

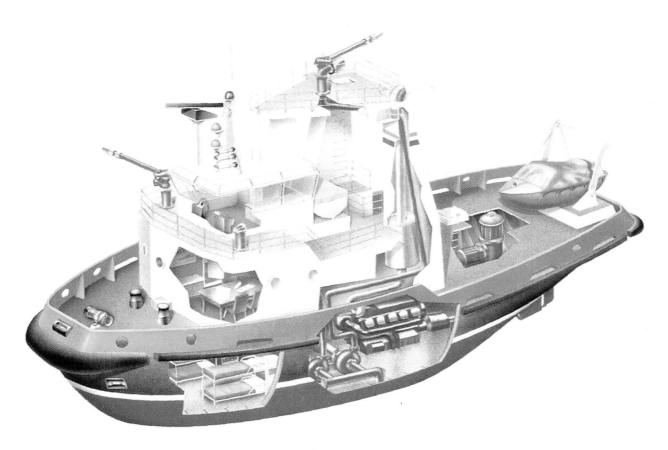

SCHOLASTIC INC.

New York Toronto London Auckland Sydney
Mexico City New Delhi Hong Kong

ISBN 0-439-21694-X

Copyright © 1997 by Aladdin Books Ltd. Copyright © 1997 U.S. text. All rights reserved. Published by Scholastic Inc., 555 Broadway, New York, NY 10012, by arrangement with Copper Beech Books, an imprint of The Millbrook Press. SCHOLASTIC and associated logos are trademarks and/or registered trademarks of Scholastic Inc.

12 11 10 9 8 7 6 5 4 3 2 1   0 1 2 3 4 5/0

Printed and bound in Canada
3 2 1 CP 00 01 02

First Scholastic printing,
September 2000

Editor
Jon Richards
Consultant
Steve Allman
Design
David West Children's Books Design
Designer
Robert Perry
Illustrators
Simon Tegg & Graham White
Picture Research
Brooks Krikler Research

CONTENTS

INTRODUCTION

Fires can be very dangerous. All over the world, men and women are specially trained to fight fires in all kinds of places.  These can be far out at sea, up tall buildings, or deep in forests. Fire fighters are also involved in other types of emergency. They 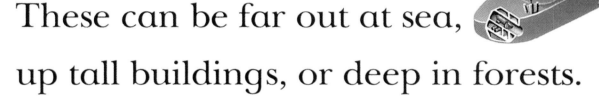 often have to rescue people trapped underground and even deal with flooding.

Ladders
The truck carries ladders. These are used to rescue people from high buildings – or to get a cat out of a tree!

Water outlet
Firefighters attach hoses to the water outlets. These are found all over the fire engine.

Equipment
The fire engine carries hoses, lights, first-aid equipment, breathing equipment (*see* page 16), and firefighters' axes.

Control panel
The control panel operates the pump that pushes water along the hoses.

FIRE ENGINE
Fire engines race down streets to get to a blaze. Their lights are flashing and sirens are blaring to clear a path through traffic.

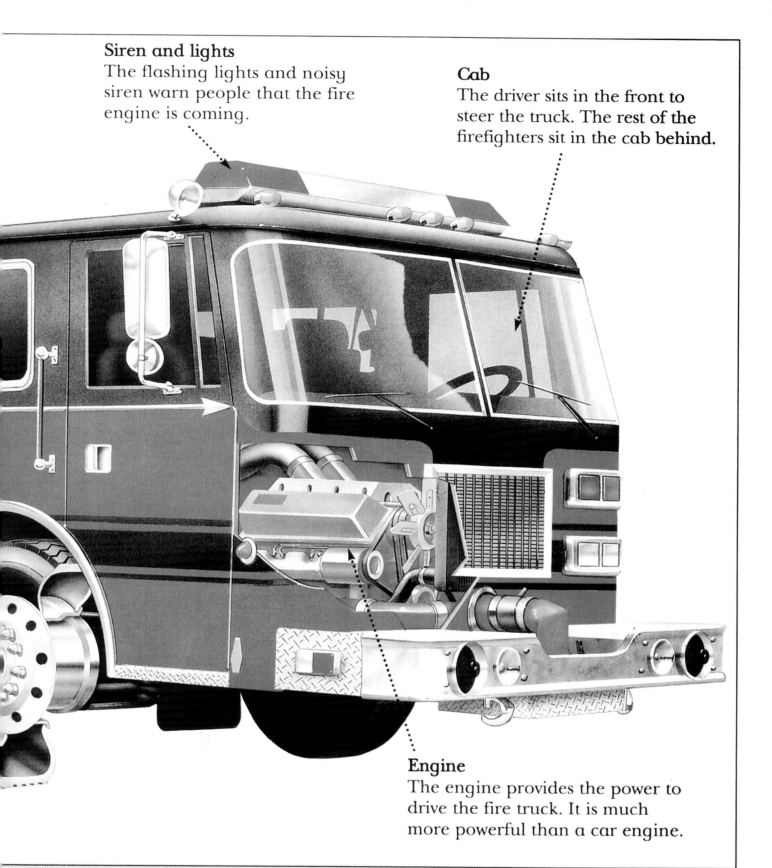

Siren and lights
The flashing lights and noisy siren warn people that the fire engine is coming.

Cab
The driver sits in the front to steer the truck. The rest of the firefighters sit in the **cab behind.**

Engine
The engine provides the power to drive the fire truck. It is much more powerful than a car engine.

The truck carries a team of firefighters. It also holds all the equipment they need to cope with many situations. This includes a big tank full of water. This holds enough water to fill over 40 bathtubs! The water is pumped out through the hoses.

Fire trucks come in

Steam engine

Early fire trucks were powered by steam (*left* and *below*). Water was heated in a boiler to produce steam. This gave the truck's pump the power to push water through the hoses.

Seat

Boiler

Wheel

1863

all shapes and sizes.

Today's trucks

This tiny fire engine (*left*) carries ladders, hoses, and two firefighters. It can get to fires down very narrow streets.

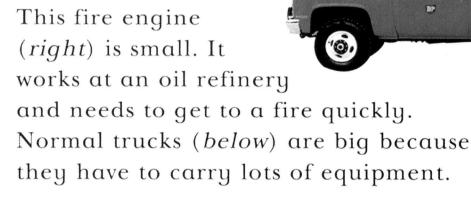

This fire engine (*right*) is small. It works at an oil refinery and needs to get to a fire quickly. Normal trucks (*below*) are big because they have to carry lots of equipment.

Turntable

The ladder is attached to a turntable. This can spin the ladder in a complete circle. The end of the ladder can also move up and down.

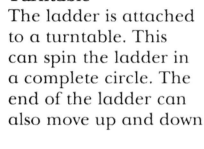

Stabilizer

These special legs stop the fire truck from falling over when the ladder is used.

AERIAL LADDER

Sometimes, firefighters need to reach fires in high places. To do this they use a long ladder.

Ladder
When the truck has got to the fire, the ladder extends to reach the flames.

Rear cab
From here, a firefighter can steer the wheels at the back. This helps the fire truck to turn very tight corners.

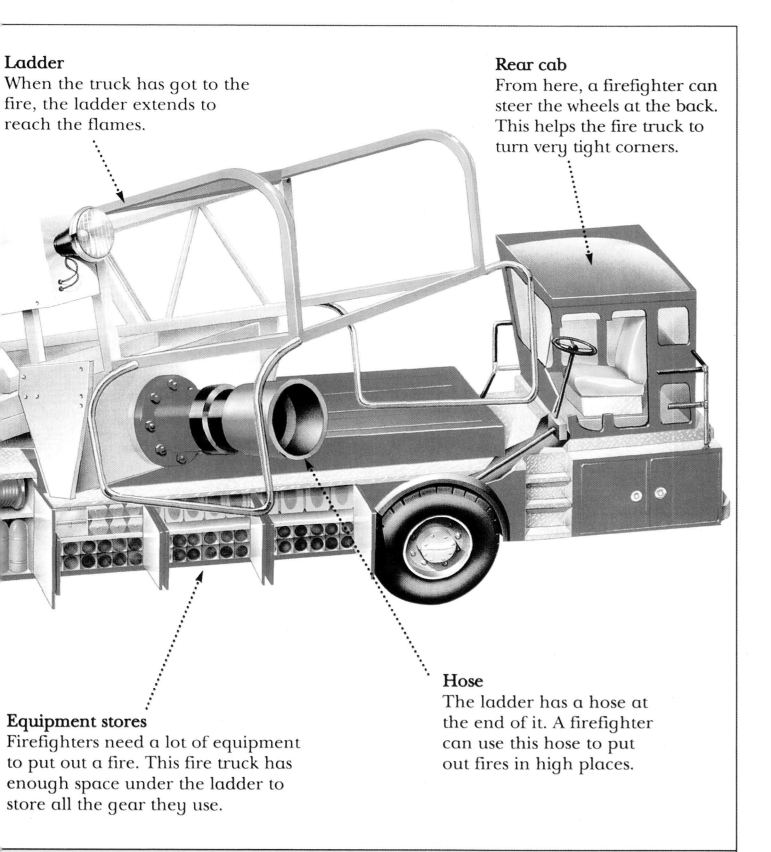

Equipment stores
Firefighters need a lot of equipment to put out a fire. This fire truck has enough space under the ladder to store all the gear they use.

Hose
The ladder has a hose at the end of it. A firefighter can use this hose to put out fires in high places.

This fire truck has a very long ladder. It is as tall as 20 people standing on top of each other! There is also a cab where the firefighters can sit. Even though it is very long, this fire truck can drive down winding streets because its back can swing.

Firefighters can get

Ladder rescue

People can get trapped in tall burning buildings. To rescue them, firefighters climb up a long ladder and help the people back down to safety (*left*).

High hoses

The hose on the end of a ladder lets firefighters spray water at flames that are far beyond the range of hoses on the ground (*below*).

Dropping in

Sometimes, even the longest ladder is not long enough. If this happens, firefighters may have to climb down the side of a building to reach a blaze (*above*).

to very high places.

Platform

Firefighter
standing on a
platform

Going up...

This fire truck (*right*) does not
have a ladder. Instead, it has a
platform on the end of a long
arm. This can reach as high as an
aerial ladder (*see* page 9).

Cab

Stabilizer

KING EDWARD SCHOOL

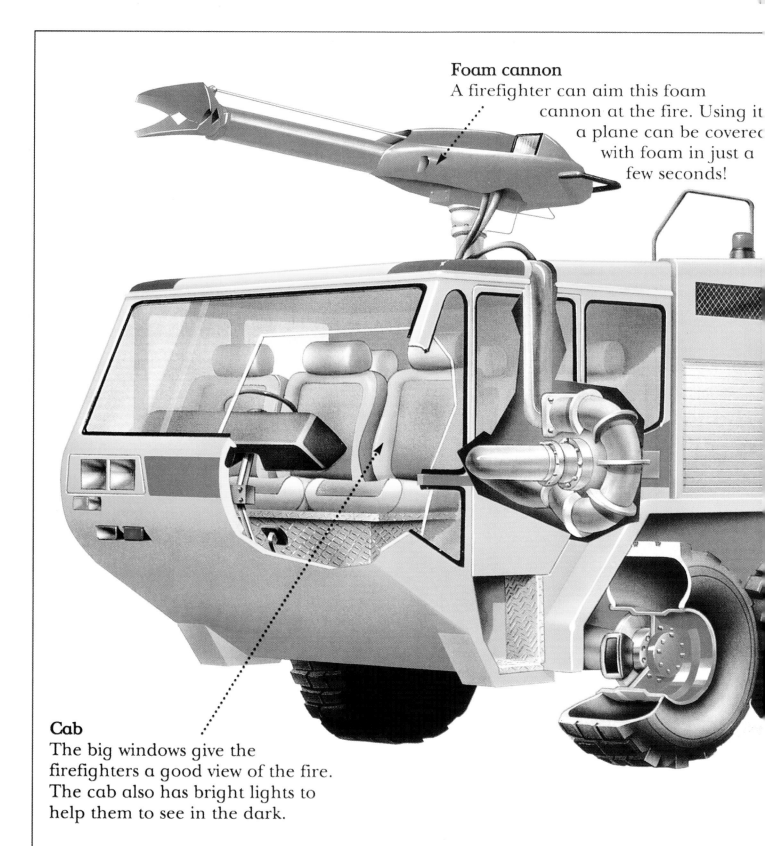

Foam cannon
A firefighter can aim this foam cannon at the fire. Using it a plane can be covered with foam in just a few seconds!

Cab
The big windows give the firefighters a good view of the fire. The cab also has bright lights to help them to see in the dark.

AIRPORT TRUCK
Fires at airports can be very dangerous. Disasters can happen in just a few seconds because aircraft fuel burns very easily.

Foam tank
Foam is stored in a huge tank inside the airport truck. From here, a powerful pump forces foam out through the foam cannon.

Engine
The engine is very powerful. It has to drive the truck at high speed and power the pump.

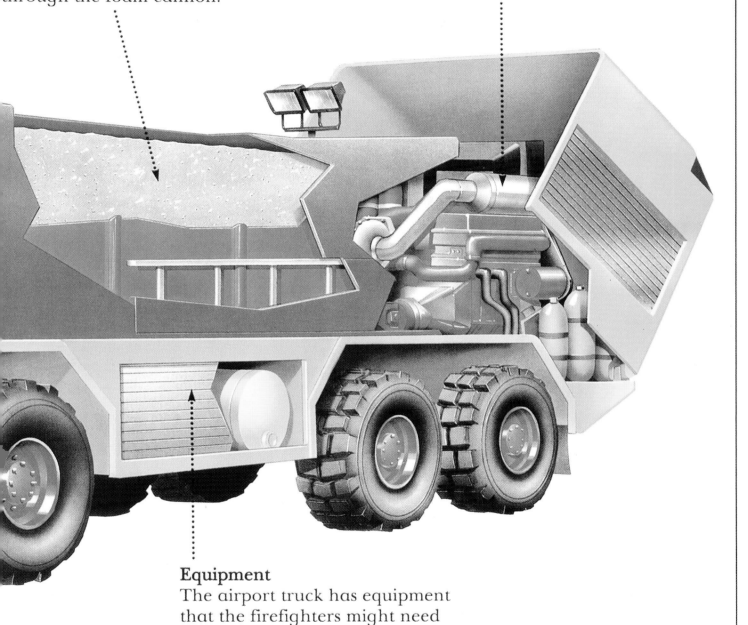

Equipment
The airport truck has equipment that the firefighters might need to rescue people from a burning plane. This includes ladders and breathing equipment.

When it arrives at a fire, the airport truck covers the blaze with a thick blanket of foam. Foam is used because water would not stop aircraft fuel from burning. The truck is always on alert, because planes are always landing at busy airports.

Different emergencies

Off-road trucks

This fire truck (*left*) can drive over rough ground. It carries a small water tank. It also has a pump that can take water from lakes or ponds.

Rescue truck

Not all emergencies are fires. This truck (*right*) has a crane to lift heavy objects. It also carries equipment to rescue people trapped in cars or even underground.

Shine a light!

This fire truck (*left*) has very bright lights. These are attached to a pole that can be raised high above the truck. This helps firefighters to see during an emergency.

need different trucks.

Crane

Command cab

Some fires are very big and need many firefighters to put them out. To direct such operations, a fire chief uses a special truck (*below*). This has a cab at the rear that acts as a command center.

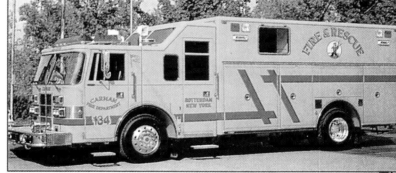

Stabilizer

Extra foam

For very big fires, extra foam may be needed. The foam carrier (*right*) carries enough spare foam to help put out the largest fires.

What it takes to

On standby

A lot of a firefighter's time is spent waiting for the next emergency. If the alarm sounds when they are eating (*left*), they have to leave their food.

Into action

Firefighters need to act quickly when the alarm sounds. Sometimes, they slide down a pole (*right*) to get to their fire trucks as quickly as possible. Every second counts!

Safe breathing

Firefighters protect themselves from smoke and fumes by wearing equipment (*left*) that gives them air to breathe.

be a firefighter.

Cleaning up

Sometimes, firefighters don't have to tackle a blaze. They may have to clean up some dangerous chemicals. To do this, they wear special suits (*left*).

Be prepared

After an emergency, firefighters have to clean and check all their equipment (*right*). They then get ready for the next alarm...

Cab
The front cab is equipped with sirens, flashing lights, and a radio. It can carry three firefighters and the driver.

Equipment
There are fire extinguishers and breathing equipment in the front cab. It also holds stretchers and a first-aid kit.

Tracks
Instead of wheels, this truck has tracks. These help it to drive over very rough ground.

TRACKED TRUCK
This truck is used to get to fires in hard-to-reach places. It can drive through a muddy field, and even travel through rivers!

Foam tank
The rear cab holds a large tank. This contains foam that the firefighters use to put out a blaze.

More equipment
The rear cab holds rescue equipment, ladders, a pump, and some hoses.

However, the ground may be too rough even for this truck. If this happens, it can be picked up and flown to a fire by helicopter.

Although they are small, the cabs of the truck can carry a team of firefighters and the equipment they need to tackle a blaze.

Fighting fires in

Guarding the tunnel

Specially built fire trucks (*right*) are used in the Channel Tunnel, which runs between England and France. These drive down a rescue tunnel to reach a fire on a train.

Fire suit

Very hot fires need special safety gear to fight them. This suit (*above left*) protects firefighters from high-temperature fires.

Oil-well fire

At an oil-well fire, firefighters put up barriers to protect themselves (*left*). When they stand behind them, they are shielded from the heat of the flames.

strange places.

Fire marshal

Racing cars can catch fire easily because they carry lots of fuel. As a result, car races have their own special firefighters (*below*). If there is a fire, they will put out the flames and rescue the driver.

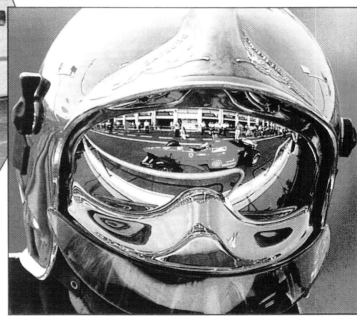

Robot fire fighter

This robot fire fighter (*right*) is used to get to fires that human firefighters couldn't reach. These could be in very small spaces or in places too dangerous for people.

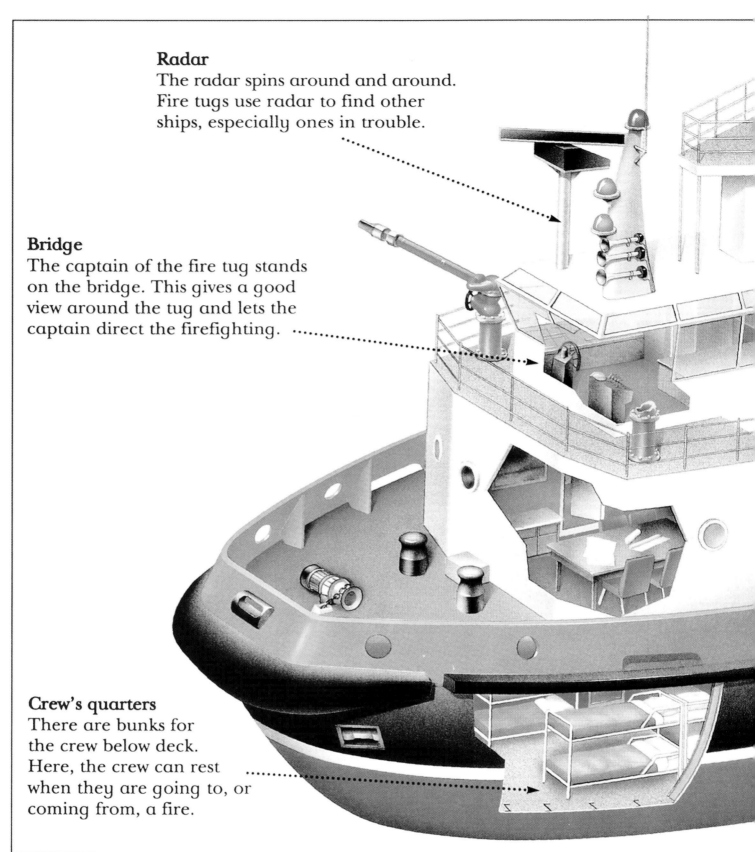

Radar
The radar spins around and around. Fire tugs use radar to find other ships, especially ones in trouble.

Bridge
The captain of the fire tug stands on the bridge. This gives a good view around the tug and lets the captain direct the firefighting.

Crew's quarters
There are bunks for the crew below deck. Here, the crew can rest when they are going to, or coming from, a fire.

FIRE TUG
Fire tugs fight fires on ships and oil rigs. They also tackle blazes that are on land at ports, harbors, and along rivers.

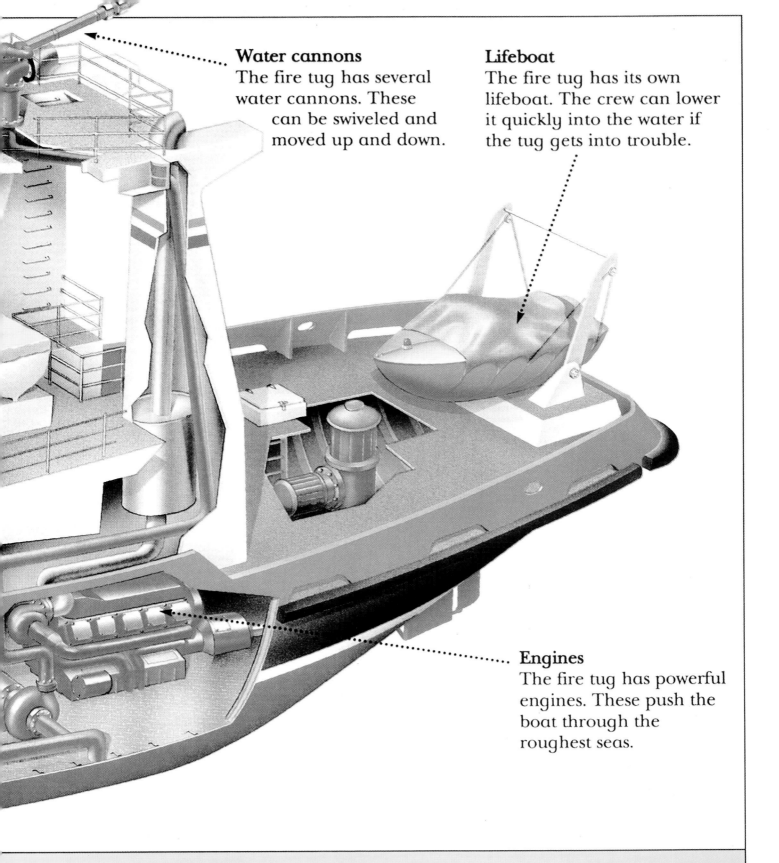

Water cannons
The fire tug has several water cannons. These can be swiveled and moved up and down.

Lifeboat
The fire tug has its own lifeboat. The crew can lower it quickly into the water if the tug gets into trouble.

Engines
The fire tug has powerful engines. These push the boat through the roughest seas.

The captain guides the boat close to the fire. The tug then pumps seawater or river water out through its water cannons.

These throw out massive jets of water that spray over long distances – up to the length of a football field!

Fires at sea can be

Support at sea

This huge craft (*right*) is called an Emergency Support Vessel (ESV). It is used to fight serious fires on oil rigs. It has helicopters to rescue people and cranes to lift objects out of the water.

Crane

Water hose

Lifeboat

Water cannons

The ESV is equipped with water cannons (*left*). These special hoses are similar to those on a fire tug (*see* pages 22-23).

Fuel

very dangerous.

Oil-rig fires

Fires on oil rigs (*left*) are very fierce. This is because the oil and gas rushes up from the seabed very quickly. This makes the fire very difficult to put out.

Helicopter

Powerful jets

The huge jets of water from a fire tug's cannons show how powerful its pumps are (*right*).

Propeller

Coast guard

When a fire occurs on a small boat, the coast guard may respond to the alarm (*left*). They have fast boats that can rescue people before a blaze gets out of control.

Fuel tanks
The aircraft carries fuel in tanks that are in its wings.

Engine
This water bomber has four engines. They are powerful enough to lift the plane when it is carrying water.

Water tanks
Water is carried in huge tanks. These are carried in the water bomber's body.

Cabin
The flight crew sit in the cabin. Behind this are bunks where they can rest.

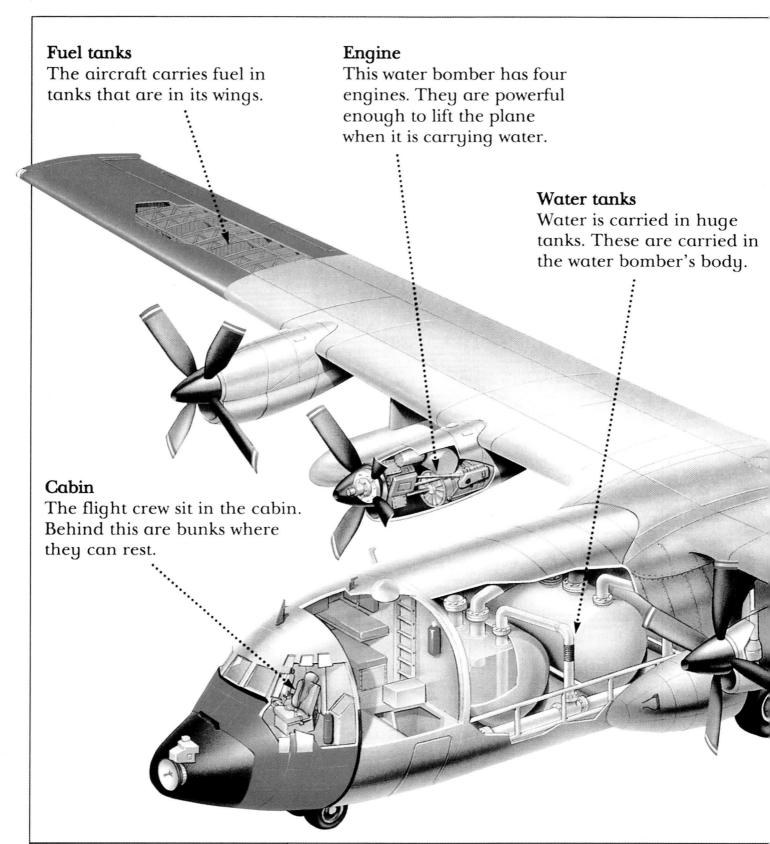

WATER BOMBER

A water bomber is an aircraft that can drop water on a fire. It is used to fight forest fires, especially in areas that are hard to reach.

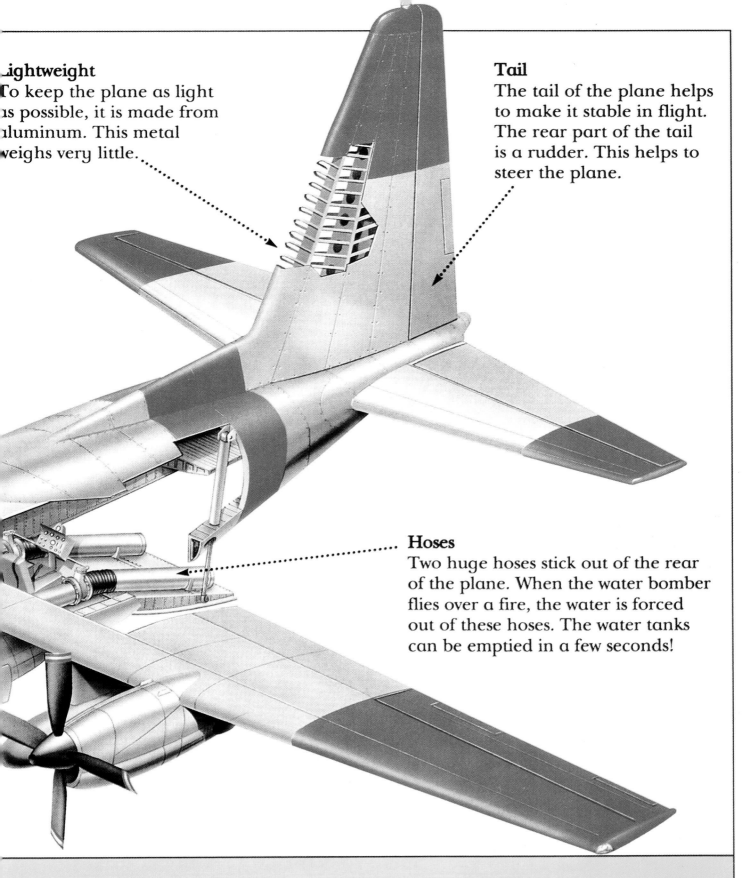

Lightweight
To keep the plane as light as possible, it is made from aluminum. This metal weighs very little.

Tail
The tail of the plane helps to make it stable in flight. The rear part of the tail is a rudder. This helps to steer the plane.

Hoses
Two huge hoses stick out of the rear of the plane. When the water bomber flies over a fire, the water is forced out of these hoses. The water tanks can be emptied in a few seconds!

reach. The aircraft flies low over a fire. With one pass, the plane can spray water over a large area of burning woodland.

The water bomber then returns to its airfield. Here, it refills its tanks with more water, before flying back to fight the fire.

There are many ways

Jumping into fires

Some firefighters are trained to parachute close to forest fires (*left*). This is useful when they are needed in a hurry at fires that are hard to reach.

Beating fires

Firefighters often try to beat out a forest fire (*below*). This is a good way to fight fires where no water is available.

Starting fires

Some fires are started deliberately (*above*). By burning forest scrub in a controlled way, firefighters can prevent serious forest fires from spreading.

to fight forest fires.

Helicopters

Helicopters can hover over the site of a fire. They drop water from a bucket which they carry beneath (*right*).

Water bucket

Forest truck

Special trucks carry firefighters to forest fires (*right*). They are built to drive over rough ground.

Fantastic Facts

• The first organized fire brigade was in ancient Rome. The firefighters were equipped with hand pumps, ladders, buckets, and pickaxes. They also had blankets to protect them from heat.

• In 1982, a fire in Borneo lasted for 10 months. It was only put out when heavy rain started to fall.

• In the summer of 1988, a forest fire at Yellowstone National Park, Wyoming, burned about half the park's area. At one time, nearly 9,500 firefighters were used to tackle the blaze.

• Smoke kills more people than fire itself. This is why breathing equipment is so important in helping to fight fires and rescue people trapped in a blaze.

Glossary

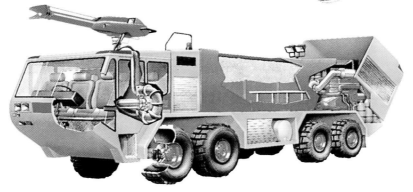

Aerial ladder

A fire truck that can be steered from the rear as well as the front.

Breathing equipment

A device that supplies air to a face mask worn by firefighters. This lets them breathe in a smoke-filled room.

Coast guard

An organization that watches the coastline to prevent accidents and smuggling.

Emergency Support Vessel (ESV)

A huge, floating platform that is used to fight fires on oil rigs.

Siren

A device attached to a vehicle that makes a wailing sound. This warns people that firefighters are coming.

Track

A loop that runs around wheels, helping a vehicle over rough ground.

Turntable

The base on which the ladder rests. It allows it to turn in a circle.

Water cannon

A special device attached to a fire tug or ESV. It is used to point a jet of water at a fire.

Index

PHOTO CREDITS
Abbreviations; t-top, m-middle, b-bottom, r-right, l-left

Pages 4, 10b, 16 both, 17t, 20m, 28b & 29b – Shout Pictures. 6t – Hulton Getty Collection. 7tl – Rex Features. 7tr, 11, 14 both, 15b & 18 – Angloco Ltd. 7b, 8 & 15m – Pierce Manufacturing. 10t, 24 & 25m – Eye Ubiquitous. 10m, 12, 20b, 20-21, 21b, 22, 25t & b, 26, 28t & 28-29 – Frank Spooner Pictures. 16b – Spectrum Color Library. 17b – Science Photo Library. 21m – Empics.